Fuck it

2022 Planner
for Sarcastically Gifted Women

This belongs to

_____

_____

Contents

Goals & Shit List

2022 Bucket List

Fucket Bucket to make sure you don't waste your precious fucks

Insults & Comebacks for dealing with assholes

2022-2023 Year-at-a-Glance Calendars

Month-at-a-Glance and Weekly/Daily planning calendars with

- Motivational swear quotes and affirmations

- US, UK and CA holidays

- *Important Shit* priority lists

- *Fucking grateful for…* gratitude prompts

- *Notes & Shit* entries

Journal pages for your *Brilliant Thoughts & Shit*

You are fucking amazing

And you need a planner that really gets that. One that's funny, fun to use and will help you get shit done.

Strong women use strong language!
Language that's as creative and colorful as you are and helps you deal with assholes and bullshit.

This planner is filled with motivational swear quotes and affirmations to help you laugh and stay positive as fuck.

You'll also find gratitude prompts and checklists to make sure you're saving your fucks for important shit.

All in a clear, easy-to-use format that will help you stay focused and avoid shitshows.

So drop those fbombs! Let those fucks fly! Be your awesome self!

And enjoy the kickass year you deserve.

Starting. Right. Fucking. Now.

Goals & shit

What goals do you want to crush with your awesomeness? Self care, relationships, hobbies, work? Your possibilities are endless.

_____

_____

_____

_____

_____

_____

_____

_____

_____

_____

_____

_____

_____

_____

_____

_____

_____

_____

_____

_____

_____

_____

2022 Bucket List

What would you fucking love to do this year? Big stuff, small stuff...
it's all good. Write that shit here and check it off when you do it.

_____

_____

_____

_____

_____

_____

_____

_____

_____

_____

_____

_____

_____

_____

_____

_____

_____

_____

_____

_____

_____

_____

_____

Fucket Bucket

Toxic people, negative thoughts and other
shit that won't get your precious fucks.

_____

_____

_____

_____

_____

_____

_____

_____

_____

_____

_____

_____

_____

_____

_____

_____

_____

_____

_____

_____

Insults & Comebacks

Assholes are everywhere. With this handy list of putdowns, you'll never be at a loss for words. There's room to add more favorites.

I'd agree with you but then we'd both be fucking wrong.

Are you always this stupid? Or is today a special occasion?

You make me wish I had more middle fingers.

Why is it acceptable for you to be an asshole but not for me to point it out?

You look like a million I-don't-give-a-fucks.

If you say you don't like me and still watch everything I do... bitch, you're a fan.

I'm jealous of everyone who hasn't met you.

Karma's only a bitch if you are. So brace yourself.

Impressive. You have even more shit coming from your mouth than your ass.

Great news. Size does matter and you are an enormous dick.

If you find me offensive, then I suggest you stop finding me.

Whoever told you to be yourself gave you bad advice.

When I said, "How fucking stupid can you be?"... it wasn't a challenge.

I'm not insulting you. I'm describing you.

You don't have to repeat yourself. I ignored you fine the first time.

Keep rolling your eyes. Maybe you'll find your brain back there.

I just baked you some shut-the-fuckupcakes.

I didn't mean to push your buttons. I was just looking for mute.

You're not as bad as people say. You're MUCH worse.

You're about as useful as a knitted condom.

_____

_____

_____

_____

_____

2022

January

S	M	T	W	T	F	S
						1
2	3	4	5	6	7	8
9	10	11	12	13	14	15
16	17	18	19	20	21	22
23	24	25	26	27	28	29
30	31					

February

S	M	T	W	T	F	S
		1	2	3	4	5
6	7	8	9	10	11	12
13	14	15	16	17	18	19
20	21	22	23	24	25	26
27	28					

March

S	M	T	W	T	F	S
		1	2	3	4	5
6	7	8	9	10	11	12
13	14	15	16	17	18	19
20	21	22	23	24	25	26
27	28	29	30	31		

April

S	M	T	W	T	F	S
					1	2
3	4	5	6	7	8	9
10	11	12	13	14	15	16
17	18	19	20	21	22	23
24	25	26	27	28	29	30

May

S	M	T	W	T	F	S
1	2	3	4	5	6	7
8	9	10	11	12	13	14
15	16	17	18	19	20	21
22	23	24	25	26	27	28
29	30	31				

June

S	M	T	W	T	F	S
			1	2	3	4
5	6	7	8	9	10	11
12	13	14	15	16	17	18
19	20	21	22	23	24	25
26	27	28	29	30		

July

S	M	T	W	T	F	S
					1	2
3	4	5	6	7	8	9
10	11	12	13	14	15	16
17	18	19	20	21	22	23
24	25	26	27	28	29	30
31						

August

S	M	T	W	T	F	S
	1	2	3	4	5	6
7	8	9	10	11	12	13
14	15	16	17	18	19	20
21	22	23	24	25	26	27
28	29	30	31			

September

S	M	T	W	T	F	S
				1	2	3
4	5	6	7	8	9	10
11	12	13	14	15	16	17
18	19	20	21	22	23	24
25	26	27	28	29	30	

October

S	M	T	W	T	F	S
						1
2	3	4	5	6	7	8
9	10	11	12	13	14	15
16	17	18	19	20	21	22
23	24	25	26	27	28	29
30	31					

November

S	M	T	W	T	F	S
		1	2	3	4	5
6	7	8	9	10	11	12
13	14	15	16	17	18	19
20	21	22	23	24	25	26
27	28	29	30			

December

S	M	T	W	T	F	S
				1	2	3
4	5	6	7	8	9	10
11	12	13	14	15	16	17
18	19	20	21	22	23	24
25	26	27	28	29	30	31

2023

January

S	M	T	W	T	F	S
1	2	3	4	5	6	7
8	9	10	11	12	13	14
15	16	17	18	19	20	21
22	23	24	25	26	27	28
29	30	31				

February

S	M	T	W	T	F	S
			1	2	3	4
5	6	7	8	9	10	11
12	13	14	15	16	17	18
19	20	21	22	23	24	25
26	27	28				

March

S	M	T	W	T	F	S
			1	2	3	4
5	6	7	8	9	10	11
12	13	14	15	16	17	18
19	20	21	22	23	24	25
26	27	28	29	30	31	

April

S	M	T	W	T	F	S
						1
2	3	4	5	6	7	8
9	10	11	12	13	14	15
16	17	18	19	20	21	22
23	24	25	26	27	28	29
30						

May

S	M	T	W	T	F	S
	1	2	3	4	5	6
7	8	9	10	11	12	13
14	15	16	17	18	19	20
21	22	23	24	25	26	27
28	29	30	31			

June

S	M	T	W	T	F	S
				1	2	3
4	5	6	7	8	9	10
11	12	13	14	15	16	17
18	19	20	21	22	23	24
25	26	27	28	29	30	

July

S	M	T	W	T	F	S
						1
2	3	4	5	6	7	8
9	10	11	12	13	14	15
16	17	18	19	20	21	22
23	24	25	26	27	28	29
30	31					

August

S	M	T	W	T	F	S
		1	2	3	4	5
6	7	8	9	10	11	12
13	14	15	16	17	18	19
20	21	22	23	24	25	26
27	28	29	30	31		

September

S	M	T	W	T	F	S
					1	2
3	4	5	6	7	8	9
10	11	12	13	14	15	16
17	18	19	20	21	22	23
24	25	26	27	28	29	30

October

S	M	T	W	T	F	S
1	2	3	4	5	6	7
8	9	10	11	12	13	14
15	16	17	18	19	20	21
22	23	24	25	26	27	28
29	30	31				

November

S	M	T	W	T	F	S
			1	2	3	4
5	6	7	8	9	10	11
12	13	14	15	16	17	18
19	20	21	22	23	24	25
26	27	28	29	30		

December

S	M	T	W	T	F	S
					1	2
3	4	5	6	7	8	9
10	11	12	13	14	15	16
17	18	19	20	21	22	23
24	25	26	27	28	29	30
31						

December 2021-January 2022

27 MONDAY	28 TUESDAY	29 WEDNESDAY

Important as *fuck*

Fucking grateful for...

Out with the old shit. In with the new awesome.

30 THURSDAY

_____
_____
_____
_____
_____
_____
_____
_____
_____
_____
_____
_____

- ○ _____
- ○ _____
- ○ _____
- ○ _____
- ○ _____
- ○ _____
- ○ _____
- ○ _____
- ○ _____

31 FRIDAY

_____
_____
_____
_____
_____
_____
_____
_____
_____
_____

- ○ _____
- ○ _____
- ○ _____
- ○ _____
- ○ _____
- ○ _____
- ○ _____
- ○ _____
- ○ _____

1 SATURDAY
New Year's Day

_____
_____
_____
_____

- ○ _____
- ○ _____
- ○ _____

2 SUNDAY

_____
_____
_____
_____
_____

- ○ _____
- ○ _____
- ○ _____

Notes and shit

_____
_____
_____

JANUARY 2022

Sunday	Monday	Tuesday	Wednesday
2	3	4	5
9	10	11	12
16	17 Martin Luther King Jr. Day (US)	18	19
23	24	25	26
30	31		

Make 2022 your bitch

Thursday	Friday	Saturday	Important shit
		1 New Year's Day	_____
			_____
6	7	8	_____
			_____
13	14	15	_____
			_____
20	21	22	_____
			_____
27	28	29	_____

December 2021

S	M	T	W	T	F	S
			1	2	3	4
5	6	7	8	9	10	11
12	13	14	15	16	17	18
19	20	21	22	23	24	25
26	27	28	29	30	31	

February 2022

S	M	T	W	T	F	S
		1	2	3	4	5
6	7	8	9	10	11	12
13	14	15	16	17	18	19
20	21	22	23	24	25	26
27	28					

January 2022

Important as *fuck*

Fucking grateful for...

Inhale the good shit. Exhale the bullshit.

6 THURSDAY

_____
_____
_____
_____
_____
_____
_____
_____
_____
_____
_____
_____

○ _____
○ _____
○ _____
○ _____
○ _____
○ _____
○ _____
○ _____
○ _____

7 FRIDAY

_____
_____
_____
_____
_____
_____
_____
_____
_____
_____
_____
_____

○ _____
○ _____
○ _____
○ _____
○ _____
○ _____
○ _____
○ _____
○ _____

8 SATURDAY

_____
_____
_____
_____
○ _____
○ _____
○ _____

9 SUNDAY

_____
_____
_____
_____
_____
○ _____
○ _____
○ _____

Notes and shit

_____
_____
_____

January 2022

10 MONDAY	11 TUESDAY	12 WEDNESDAY
_____	_____	_____
_____	_____	_____
_____	_____	_____
_____	_____	_____
_____	_____	_____
_____	_____	_____
_____	_____	_____
_____	_____	_____
_____	_____	_____
_____	_____	_____
_____	_____	_____
_____	_____	_____

- ○ _____
- ○ _____
- ○ _____
- ○ _____
- ○ _____
- ○ _____
- ○ _____
- ○ _____
- ○ _____

Important as *fuck*

_____
_____
_____

Fucking grateful for...

_____
_____
_____

Keep your head high and your middle finger higher

13 THURSDAY **14 FRIDAY** **15 SATURDAY**

16 SUNDAY

Notes and shit

January 2022

17 MONDAY	18 TUESDAY	19 WEDNESDAY
Martin Luther King Jr. Day (US)		

Important as *fuck*

Fucking grateful for...

Do more of what makes you fucking happy

20 THURSDAY

- ○
- ○
- ○
- ○
- ○
- ○
- ○
- ○
- ○

21 FRIDAY

- ○
- ○
- ○
- ○
- ○
- ○
- ○
- ○
- ○

22 SATURDAY

- ○
- ○
- ○

23 SUNDAY

- ○
- ○
- ○

Notes and shit

January 2022

You are a fucking unicorn.

24 MONDAY	25 TUESDAY	26 WEDNESDAY
_____	_____	_____
_____	_____	_____
_____	_____	_____
_____	_____	_____
_____	_____	_____
_____	_____	_____
_____	_____	_____
_____	_____	_____
_____	_____	_____
_____	_____	_____
_____	_____	_____
_____	_____	_____
○ _____	○ _____	○ _____
○ _____	○ _____	○ _____
○ _____	○ _____	○ _____
○ _____	○ _____	○ _____
○ _____	○ _____	○ _____
○ _____	○ _____	○ _____
○ _____	○ _____	○ _____
○ _____	○ _____	○ _____
○ _____	○ _____	○ _____

Important as fuck

_____
_____
_____

Fucking grateful for...

_____
_____
_____

Just resist the urge to stab assholes with your head.

27 THURSDAY

_____
_____
_____
_____
_____
_____
_____
_____
_____
_____
_____
_____

- ◯ _____
- ◯ _____
- ◯ _____
- ◯ _____
- ◯ _____
- ◯ _____
- ◯ _____
- ◯ _____
- ◯ _____

28 FRIDAY

_____
_____
_____
_____
_____
_____
_____
_____
_____
_____

- ◯ _____
- ◯ _____
- ◯ _____
- ◯ _____
- ◯ _____
- ◯ _____
- ◯ _____
- ◯ _____
- ◯ _____

29 SATURDAY

_____
_____
_____
_____
- ◯ _____
- ◯ _____
- ◯ _____

30 SUNDAY

_____
_____
_____
_____
_____
- ◯ _____
- ◯ _____
- ◯ _____

Notes and shit

_____
_____
_____

FEBRUARY 2022

Sunday	Monday	Tuesday	Wednesday
		1	2
6	7	8	9
13	14 Valentine's Day	15	16
20	21 President's Day (US)	22	23
27	28		

Fuck perfect

Thursday	Friday	Saturday	Important shit
3	4	5	
10	11	12	
17	18	19	
24	25	26	

January

S	M	T	W	T	F	S
						1
2	3	4	5	6	7	8
9	10	11	12	13	14	15
16	17	18	19	20	21	22
23	24	25	26	27	28	29
30	31					

March

S	M	T	W	T	F	S
		1	2	3	4	5
6	7	8	9	10	11	12
13	14	15	16	17	18	19
20	21	22	23	24	25	26
27	28	29	30	31		

January-February 2022

31 MONDAY	1 TUESDAY	2 WEDNESDAY
_____	_____	_____
_____	_____	_____
_____	_____	_____
_____	_____	_____
_____	_____	_____
_____	_____	_____
_____	_____	_____
_____	_____	_____
_____	_____	_____
_____	_____	_____
_____	_____	_____
_____	_____	_____
○ _____	○ _____	○ _____
○ _____	○ _____	○ _____
○ _____	○ _____	○ _____
○ _____	○ _____	○ _____
○ _____	○ _____	○ _____
○ _____	○ _____	○ _____
○ _____	○ _____	○ _____
○ _____	○ _____	○ _____
○ _____	○ _____	○ _____

Important as *fuck*

_____
_____
_____

Fucking grateful for...

_____
_____
_____

Be kind as fuck to yourself

3 THURSDAY

_____
_____
_____
_____
_____
_____
_____
_____
_____
_____
_____

- ○ _____
- ○ _____
- ○ _____
- ○ _____
- ○ _____
- ○ _____
- ○ _____
- ○ _____
- ○ _____

4 FRIDAY

_____
_____
_____
_____
_____
_____
_____
_____
_____
_____
_____

- ○ _____
- ○ _____
- ○ _____
- ○ _____
- ○ _____
- ○ _____
- ○ _____
- ○ _____
- ○ _____

5 SATURDAY

_____
_____
_____
_____
_____

- ○ _____
- ○ _____
- ○ _____

6 SUNDAY

_____
_____
_____
_____
_____

- ○ _____
- ○ _____
- ○ _____

Notes and shit

_____
_____
_____

February 2022

|| 7 MONDAY | 8 TUESDAY | 9 WEDNESDAY |

Important as *fuck*

Fucking grateful for...

Your inner critic is a total bitch. Ignore her.

10 THURSDAY

_____
_____
_____
_____
_____
_____
_____
_____
_____
_____
_____
_____
_____
_____
○ _____
○ _____
○ _____
○ _____
○ _____
○ _____
○ _____
○ _____
○ _____

11 FRIDAY

_____
_____
_____
_____
_____
_____
_____
_____
_____
_____
_____
_____
○ _____
○ _____
○ _____
○ _____
○ _____
○ _____
○ _____
○ _____
○ _____

12 SATURDAY

_____
_____
_____
_____
○ _____
○ _____
○ _____

13 SUNDAY

_____
_____
_____
_____
_____
○ _____
○ _____
○ _____

Notes and shit

_____
_____
_____

February 2022

Be yourself...

14 MONDAY	15 TUESDAY	16 WEDNESDAY
Valentine's Day		

○ ──────────────
○ ──────────────
○ ──────────────
○ ──────────────
○ ──────────────
○ ──────────────
○ ──────────────
○ ──────────────
○ ──────────────

Important as fuck

────────────────
────────────────
────────────────

Fucking grateful for...

────────────────
────────────────
────────────────

People don't have to like it and you don't have to give a fuck

17 THURSDAY	18 FRIDAY	19 SATURDAY

○
○
○

20 SUNDAY

○
○
○
○
○
○
○
○
○

○
○
○
○
○
○
○
○
○

○
○
○

Notes and shit

February 2022

21 MONDAY	22 TUESDAY	23 WEDNESDAY
President's Day (US)		

Important as *fuck*

Fucking grateful for...

A grateful heart is a magnet for more good shit

24 THURSDAY

_____
_____
_____
_____
_____
_____
_____
_____
_____
_____
_____

○ _____
○ _____
○ _____
○ _____
○ _____
○ _____
○ _____
○ _____
○ _____

25 FRIDAY

_____
_____
_____
_____
_____
_____
_____
_____
_____
_____
_____

○ _____
○ _____
○ _____
○ _____
○ _____
○ _____
○ _____
○ _____
○ _____

26 SATURDAY

_____
_____
_____
_____
○ _____
○ _____
○ _____

27 SUNDAY

_____
_____
_____
_____
○ _____
○ _____
○ _____

Notes and shit

_____
_____
_____

MARCH 2022

Sunday	Monday	Tuesday	Wednesday
		1	2
6	7	8 International Women's Day	9
13	14	15	16
20	21	22	23
27 Mother's Day (UK)	28	29	30

Love the fuck out of yourself

Thursday	Friday	Saturday
3	4	5
10	11	12
17 St. Patrick's Day	18	19
24	25	26
31		

Important shit

_____
_____
_____
_____
_____
_____
_____
_____
_____
_____
_____
_____
_____
_____
_____
_____
_____
_____
_____
_____
_____
_____
_____

February

S	M	T	W	T	F	S
		1	2	3	4	5
6	7	8	9	10	11	12
13	14	15	16	17	18	19
20	21	22	23	24	25	26
27	28					

April

S	M	T	W	T	F	S
					1	2
3	4	5	6	7	8	9
10	11	12	13	14	15	16
17	18	19	20	21	22	23
24	25	26	27	28	29	30

February-March 2022

28 MONDAY	1 TUESDAY	2 WEDNESDAY
_____	_____	_____
_____	_____	_____
_____	_____	_____
_____	_____	_____
_____	_____	_____
_____	_____	_____
_____	_____	_____
_____	_____	_____
_____	_____	_____
_____	_____	_____
_____	_____	_____
_____	_____	_____
○ _____	○ _____	○ _____
○ _____	○ _____	○ _____
○ _____	○ _____	○ _____
○ _____	○ _____	○ _____
○ _____	○ _____	○ _____
○ _____	○ _____	○ _____
○ _____	○ _____	○ _____
○ _____	○ _____	○ _____
○ _____	○ _____	○ _____

Important as *fuck*

_____
_____
_____

Fucking grateful for...

_____
_____
_____

May your bucket list be as long as your fuck-it list

3 THURSDAY

_____
_____
_____
_____
_____
_____
_____
_____
_____
_____
_____

○ _____
○ _____
○ _____
○ _____
○ _____
○ _____
○ _____
○ _____
○ _____

4 FRIDAY

_____
_____
_____
_____
_____
_____
_____

○ _____
○ _____
○ _____
○ _____
○ _____
○ _____
○ _____
○ _____
○ _____

5 SATURDAY

_____
_____
_____
_____

○ _____
○ _____
○ _____

6 SUNDAY

_____
_____
_____
_____

○ _____
○ _____
○ _____

Notes and shit

_____
_____
_____

March 2022

7 MONDAY	8 TUESDAY International Women's Day	9 WEDNESDAY
_____	_____	_____
_____	_____	_____
_____	_____	_____
_____	_____	_____
_____	_____	_____
_____	_____	_____
_____	_____	_____
_____	_____	_____
_____	_____	_____
_____	_____	_____
_____	_____	_____
_____	_____	_____
○ _____	○ _____	○ _____
○ _____	○ _____	○ _____
○ _____	○ _____	○ _____
○ _____	○ _____	○ _____
○ _____	○ _____	○ _____
○ _____	○ _____	○ _____
○ _____	○ _____	○ _____
○ _____	○ _____	○ _____
○ _____	○ _____	○ _____

Important as *fuck*

_____
_____
_____

Fucking grateful for...

_____
_____
_____

The first five days after the weekend are the hardest

10 THURSDAY

_____
_____
_____
_____
_____
_____
_____
_____
_____
_____
_____
_____
- ○ _____
- ○ _____
- ○ _____
- ○ _____
- ○ _____
- ○ _____
- ○ _____
- ○ _____
- ○ _____

11 FRIDAY

_____
_____
_____
_____
_____
_____
_____
_____
_____
_____
- ○ _____
- ○ _____
- ○ _____
- ○ _____
- ○ _____
- ○ _____
- ○ _____
- ○ _____
- ○ _____

12 SATURDAY

_____
_____
_____
_____
- ○ _____
- ○ _____
- ○ _____

13 SUNDAY

_____
_____
_____
_____
_____
- ○ _____
- ○ _____
- ○ _____

Notes and shit

_____
_____
_____

March 2022

14 MONDAY | 15 TUESDAY | 16 WEDNESDAY

Important as *fuck*

Fucking grateful for...

begins with a single fucking step

17 THURSDAY
St. Patrick's Day

_____
_____
_____
_____
_____
_____
_____
_____
_____
_____
_____

○ _____
○ _____
○ _____
○ _____
○ _____
○ _____
○ _____
○ _____
○ _____

18 FRIDAY

_____
_____
_____
_____
_____
_____
_____
_____
_____
_____
_____

○ _____
○ _____
○ _____
○ _____
○ _____
○ _____
○ _____
○ _____
○ _____

19 SATURDAY

_____
_____
○ _____
○ _____
○ _____

20 SUNDAY

_____
_____
_____
_____
_____
_____
○ _____
○ _____
○ _____

Notes and shit

_____
_____

March 2022

Important as fuck

Fucking grateful for...

If you can't say something nice, write that shit down

24 THURSDAY

- ○ _____
- ○ _____
- ○ _____
- ○ _____
- ○ _____
- ○ _____
- ○ _____
- ○ _____
- ○ _____

25 FRIDAY

- ○ _____
- ○ _____
- ○ _____
- ○ _____
- ○ _____
- ○ _____
- ○ _____
- ○ _____
- ○ _____

26 SATURDAY

- ○ _____
- ○ _____
- ○ _____

27 SUNDAY
Mother's Day (UK)

- ○ _____
- ○ _____
- ○ _____

Notes and shit

March-April 2022

28 MONDAY	29 TUESDAY	30 WEDNESDAY

28 MONDAY
_____
_____
_____
_____
_____
_____
_____
_____
_____
_____
_____
_____
_____

○ _____
○ _____
○ _____
○ _____
○ _____
○ _____
○ _____
○ _____
○ _____

29 TUESDAY
_____
_____
_____
_____
_____
_____
_____
_____
_____
_____
_____
_____
_____

○ _____
○ _____
○ _____
○ _____
○ _____
○ _____
○ _____
○ _____
○ _____

30 WEDNESDAY
_____
_____
_____
_____
_____
_____
_____
_____
_____
_____
_____
_____
_____

○ _____
○ _____
○ _____
○ _____
○ _____
○ _____
○ _____
○ _____
○ _____

Important as *fuck*
_____
_____
_____

Fucking grateful for...
_____
_____
_____

You are a ray of fucking sunshine

31 THURSDAY

_____
_____
_____
_____
_____
_____
_____
_____
_____
_____
_____
_____

- ○ _____
- ○ _____
- ○ _____
- ○ _____
- ○ _____
- ○ _____
- ○ _____
- ○ _____
- ○ _____

1 FRIDAY
April Fools' Day

_____
_____
_____
_____
_____
_____
_____
_____
_____
_____
_____

- ○ _____
- ○ _____
- ○ _____
- ○ _____
- ○ _____
- ○ _____
- ○ _____
- ○ _____
- ○ _____

2 SATURDAY
Ramadan begins at sundown

_____
_____
_____
_____
_____

- ○ _____
- ○ _____
- ○ _____

3 SUNDAY

_____
_____
_____
_____
_____

- ○ _____
- ○ _____
- ○ _____

Notes and shit

_____
_____
_____

APRIL 2022

Sunday	Monday	Tuesday	Wednesday
March S M T W T F S 1 2 3 4 5 6 7 8 9 10 11 12 13 14 15 16 17 18 19 20 21 22 23 24 25 26 27 28 29 30 31	**May** S M T W T F S 1 2 3 4 5 6 7 8 9 10 11 12 13 14 15 16 17 18 19 20 21 22 23 24 25 26 27 28 29 30 31		
3	4	5	6
10	11	12	13
17 Easter	18 Easter Monday (CA)	19	20
24	25	26	27

Bloom bitch

Thursday	Friday	Saturday	Important shit
	1 April Fools' Day	2 Ramadan begins at sundown	_____ _____ _____ _____
7	8	9	_____ _____ _____ _____ _____
14	15 Good Friday Passover, starts at sundown	16	_____ _____ _____ _____
21	22 Earth Day	23	_____ _____ _____ _____
28	29	30	_____ _____ _____ _____

April 2022

4 MONDAY	5 TUESDAY	6 WEDNESDAY
_____	_____	_____
_____	_____	_____
_____	_____	_____
_____	_____	_____
_____	_____	_____
_____	_____	_____
_____	_____	_____
_____	_____	_____
_____	_____	_____
_____	_____	_____
_____	_____	_____
_____	_____	_____
○ _____	○ _____	○ _____
○ _____	○ _____	○ _____
○ _____	○ _____	○ _____
○ _____	○ _____	○ _____
○ _____	○ _____	○ _____
○ _____	○ _____	○ _____
○ _____	○ _____	○ _____
○ _____	○ _____	○ _____
○ _____	○ _____	○ _____

Important as *fuck*

_____

_____

_____

Fucking grateful for...

_____

_____

_____

It's a beautiful day to get shit done

7 THURSDAY

_____
_____
_____
_____
_____
_____
_____
_____
_____
_____
_____

○ _____
○ _____
○ _____
○ _____
○ _____
○ _____
○ _____
○ _____
○ _____

8 FRIDAY

_____
_____
_____
_____
_____
_____
_____
_____
_____

○ _____
○ _____
○ _____
○ _____
○ _____
○ _____
○ _____
○ _____
○ _____

9 SATURDAY

_____
_____
_____
_____
_____
○ _____
○ _____
○ _____

10 SUNDAY

_____
_____
_____
_____
_____
○ _____
○ _____
○ _____

Notes and shit

_____
_____
_____

April 2022

Every day may not be a good day...

11 MONDAY	12 TUESDAY	13 WEDNESDAY
_____	_____	_____
_____	_____	_____
_____	_____	_____
_____	_____	_____
_____	_____	_____
_____	_____	_____
_____	_____	_____
_____	_____	_____
_____	_____	_____
_____	_____	_____
_____	_____	_____
○ _____	○ _____	○ _____
○ _____	○ _____	○ _____
○ _____	○ _____	○ _____
○ _____	○ _____	○ _____
○ _____	○ _____	○ _____
○ _____	○ _____	○ _____
○ _____	○ _____	○ _____
○ _____	○ _____	○ _____
○ _____	○ _____	○ _____

Important as *fuck*

_____

_____

_____

Fucking grateful for...

_____

_____

_____

but there's some good shit in every day.

14 THURSDAY

_____
_____
_____
_____
_____
_____
_____
_____
_____
_____
_____

○ _____
○ _____
○ _____
○ _____
○ _____
○ _____
○ _____
○ _____
○ _____

15 FRIDAY
Good Friday, Passover, begins at Sunset

_____
_____
_____
_____
_____
_____
_____
_____
_____

○ _____
○ _____
○ _____
○ _____
○ _____
○ _____
○ _____
○ _____
○ _____

16 SATURDAY

_____
_____
_____
_____
_____
○ _____
○ _____
○ _____

17 SUNDAY
Easter

_____
_____
_____
_____
_____
○ _____
○ _____
○ _____

Notes and *shit*

_____
_____
_____

April 2022

18 MONDAY	19 TUESDAY	20 WEDNESDAY
Easter Monday (CA)		

Important as fuck

Fucking grateful for...

You're not a bitch. You're a teller of unfortunate truths.

21 THURSDAY

_____
_____
_____
_____
_____
_____
_____
_____
_____
_____
_____
_____

- ○ _____
- ○ _____
- ○ _____
- ○ _____
- ○ _____
- ○ _____
- ○ _____
- ○ _____
- ○ _____

22 FRIDAY
Earth Day

_____
_____
_____
_____
_____
_____
_____
_____
_____

- ○ _____
- ○ _____
- ○ _____
- ○ _____
- ○ _____
- ○ _____
- ○ _____
- ○ _____
- ○ _____

23 SATURDAY

_____
_____
_____
_____
_____
- ○ _____
- ○ _____
- ○ _____

24 SUNDAY

_____
_____
_____
_____
_____
_____
- ○ _____
- ○ _____
- ○ _____

Notes and shit

_____
_____
_____

25 MONDAY	26 TUESDAY	27 WEDNESDAY
_____	_____	_____
_____	_____	_____
_____	_____	_____
_____	_____	_____
_____	_____	_____
_____	_____	_____
_____	_____	_____
_____	_____	_____
_____	_____	_____
_____	_____	_____
_____	_____	_____
_____	_____	_____

- ○ _____
- ○ _____
- ○ _____
- ○ _____
- ○ _____
- ○ _____
- ○ _____
- ○ _____
- ○ _____

Important as *fuck*

_____
_____
_____

Fucking grateful for...

_____
_____

Life's too short to hang out with assholes

28 THURSDAY

_____
_____
_____
_____
_____
_____
_____
_____
_____
_____
_____
_____
○ _____
○ _____
○ _____
○ _____
○ _____
○ _____
○ _____
○ _____
○ _____

29 FRIDAY

_____
_____
_____
_____
_____
_____
_____
○ _____
○ _____
○ _____
○ _____
○ _____
○ _____
○ _____
○ _____
○ _____

30 SATURDAY

_____
_____
_____
_____
_____
○ _____
○ _____
○ _____

1 SUNDAY
Labour Day (UK)

_____
_____
_____
_____
○ _____
○ _____
○ _____

Notes and shit

_____
_____
_____

MAY 2022

Sunday	Monday	Tuesday	Wednesday
1 Labour Day (UK)	2 Early May Bank Holiday (UK)	3	4
8 Mother's Day (US, CA)	9	10	11
15	16	17	18
22	23	24	25
29	30 Memorial Day (US)	31	

Let that shit go

Thursday	Friday	Saturday	Important shit
5 Cinco de Mayo (US)	6	7	_____
			_____
12	13	14	_____
			_____
19	20	21 Armed Forces Day (US)	_____
			_____
26	27	28	_____

April

S	M	T	W	T	F	S
					1	2
3	4	5	6	7	8	9
10	11	12	13	14	15	16
17	18	19	20	21	22	23
24	25	26	27	28	29	30

June

S	M	T	W	T	F	S
			1	2	3	4
5	6	7	8	9	10	11
12	13	14	15	16	17	18
19	20	21	22	23	24	25
26	27	28	29	30		

May 2022

Important as *fuck*

Fucking grateful for...

Feel the fear and do that shit anyway

5 THURSDAY

_____
_____
_____
_____
_____
_____
_____
_____
_____
_____
_____

○ _____
○ _____
○ _____
○ _____
○ _____
○ _____
○ _____
○ _____
○ _____

6 FRIDAY

_____
_____
_____
_____
_____
_____
_____
_____
_____

○ _____
○ _____
○ _____
○ _____
○ _____
○ _____
○ _____
○ _____
○ _____

7 SATURDAY

_____
_____
_____
_____
_____

○ _____
○ _____
○ _____

8 SUNDAY
Mother's Day (US, CA)

_____
_____
_____
_____

○ _____
○ _____
○ _____

Notes and *shit*

_____
_____
_____

In a world where you can be anything, be kind. . .

9 MONDAY	10 TUESDAY	11 WEDNESDAY

_____
_____
_____
_____
_____
_____
_____
_____
_____
_____
_____
_____

○ _____
○ _____
○ _____
○ _____
○ _____
○ _____
○ _____
○ _____
○ _____

Important as fuck

_____
_____
_____

Fucking grateful for...

_____
_____
_____

and kinda bitchy. You're only human after all.

12 THURSDAY

_____
_____
_____
_____
_____
_____
_____
_____
_____
_____
_____
_____

- ○ _____
- ○ _____
- ○ _____
- ○ _____
- ○ _____
- ○ _____
- ○ _____
- ○ _____
- ○ _____

13 FRIDAY

_____
_____
_____
_____
_____
_____
_____
_____
_____
_____

- ○ _____
- ○ _____
- ○ _____
- ○ _____
- ○ _____
- ○ _____
- ○ _____
- ○ _____
- ○ _____

14 SATURDAY

_____
_____
_____
- ○ _____
- ○ _____
- ○ _____

15 SUNDAY

_____
_____
_____
_____
_____
- ○ _____
- ○ _____
- ○ _____

Notes and shit

_____
_____
_____

May 2022

16 MONDAY	17 TUESDAY	18 WEDNESDAY

Important as fuck

Fucking grateful for...

Tell negative thoughts to fuck off

19 THURSDAY

20 FRIDAY

21 SATURDAY
Armed Forces Day (US)

_____
_____
_____
_____
_____
_____
_____
_____
_____
_____

○ _____
○ _____
○ _____

22 SUNDAY

○ _____
○ _____
○ _____
○ _____
○ _____
○ _____
○ _____
○ _____
○ _____

○ _____
○ _____

Notes and shit

_____
_____
_____

May 2022

23 MONDAY	24 TUESDAY	25 WEDNESDAY
_____	_____	_____
_____	_____	_____
_____	_____	_____
_____	_____	_____
_____	_____	_____
_____	_____	_____
_____	_____	_____
_____	_____	_____
_____	_____	_____
_____	_____	_____
_____	_____	_____
_____	_____	_____
○ _____	○ _____	○ _____
○ _____	○ _____	○ _____
○ _____	○ _____	○ _____
○ _____	○ _____	○ _____
○ _____	○ _____	○ _____
○ _____	○ _____	○ _____
○ _____	○ _____	○ _____
○ _____	○ _____	○ _____
○ _____	○ _____	○ _____

Important as *fuck*

Fucking grateful for...

You are bullshit proof

26 THURSDAY

_____
_____
_____
_____
_____
_____
_____
_____
_____
_____
_____

○ _____
○ _____
○ _____
○ _____
○ _____
○ _____
○ _____
○ _____
○ _____

27 FRIDAY

_____
_____
_____
_____
_____
_____
_____
_____
_____

○ _____
○ _____
○ _____
○ _____
○ _____
○ _____
○ _____
○ _____
○ _____

28 SATURDAY

_____
_____
_____
_____

○ _____
○ _____
○ _____

29 SUNDAY

_____
_____
_____
_____

○ _____
○ _____
○ _____

Notes and shit

_____
_____
_____

JUNE 2022

Sunday	Monday	Tuesday	Wednesday
			1
5	6	7	8
12	13	14 Flag Day (US)	15
19 Father's Day Juneteenth (US)	20	21	22
26	27	28	29

Aim for progress, not fucking perfection

Thursday	Friday	Saturday	Important shit
2 Spring Bank Holiday (UK)	3 Queen's Platinum Jubilee (UK)	4	
9	10	11	
16	17	18	
23	24	25	
30			

May

S	M	T	W	T	F	S
1	2	3	4	5	6	7
8	9	10	11	12	13	14
15	16	17	18	19	20	21
22	23	24	25	26	27	28
29	30	31				

July

S	M	T	W	T	F	S
					1	2
3	4	5	6	7	8	9
10	11	12	13	14	15	16
17	18	19	20	21	22	23
24	25	26	27	28	29	30
31						

May-June 2022

Important as *fuck*

Fucking grateful for...

Do epic shit. And, yes, epic naps count.

2 THURSDAY
Spring Bank Holiday (UK)

3 FRIDAY
Queen's Platinum Jubilee (UK)

4 SATURDAY

5 SUNDAY

Notes and shit

June 2022

Important as *fuck*

Fucking grateful for...

Have a fucktastic day

9 THURSDAY

_____
_____
_____
_____
_____
_____
_____
_____
_____
_____
_____
_____

- ○ _____
- ○ _____
- ○ _____
- ○ _____
- ○ _____
- ○ _____
- ○ _____
- ○ _____
- ○ _____

10 FRIDAY

_____
_____
_____
_____
_____
_____
_____
_____
_____
_____
_____

- ○ _____
- ○ _____
- ○ _____
- ○ _____
- ○ _____
- ○ _____
- ○ _____
- ○ _____
- ○ _____

11 SATURDAY

_____
_____
_____
_____
_____

- ○ _____
- ○ _____
- ○ _____

12 SUNDAY

_____
_____
_____
_____
_____
_____

- ○ _____
- ○ _____
- ○ _____

Notes and shit

_____
_____
_____

June 2022

13 MONDAY	14 TUESDAY	15 WEDNESDAY
	Flag Day (US)	

Important as *fuck*

Fucking grateful for...

You are fucking beautiful... inside and out

16 THURSDAY

17 FRIDAY

18 SATURDAY

○
○
○

19 SUNDAY
Father's Day, Juneteenth (US)

○
○
○
○
○
○
○
○
○

○
○
○
○
○
○
○
○
○

○
○
○

Notes and shit

June 2022

Important as *fuck*

Fucking grateful for...

Save your fucks for important shit

23 THURSDAY

_____
_____
_____
_____
_____
_____
_____
_____
_____
_____
_____
_____

- ○ _____
- ○ _____
- ○ _____
- ○ _____
- ○ _____
- ○ _____
- ○ _____
- ○ _____
- ○ _____

24 FRIDAY

_____
_____
_____
_____
_____
_____
_____
_____
_____

- ○ _____
- ○ _____
- ○ _____
- ○ _____
- ○ _____
- ○ _____
- ○ _____
- ○ _____
- ○ _____

25 SATURDAY

_____
_____
_____
_____
- ○ _____
- ○ _____
- ○ _____

26 SUNDAY

_____
_____
_____
_____
- ○ _____
- ○ _____
- ○ _____

Notes and shit

_____
_____
_____

JULY 2022

Sunday	Monday	Tuesday	Wednesday
3	4 Independence Day (US)	5	6
10	11	12	13
17	18	19	20
24	25	26	27
31			

Manifest that shit

Thursday	Friday	Saturday	Important shit
	1 Canada Day (CA)	2	_____
7	8	9	_____
14	15	16	_____
21	22	23	_____
28	29	30	_____

June

S	M	T	W	T	F	S
			1	2	3	4
5	6	7	8	9	10	11
12	13	14	15	16	17	18
19	20	21	22	23	24	25
26	27	28	29	30		

August

S	M	T	W	T	F	S
	1	2	3	4	5	6
7	8	9	10	11	12	13
14	15	16	17	18	19	20
21	22	23	24	25	26	27
28	29	30	31			

June-July 2022

27 MONDAY	28 TUESDAY	29 WEDNESDAY

Important as *fuck*

Fucking grateful for...

Your hobbies include having no time for this shit

30 THURSDAY

1 FRIDAY
Canada Day (CA)

2 SATURDAY

○
○
○

3 SUNDAY

○
○
○
○
○
○
○
○
○

○
○
○
○
○
○
○
○
○

○
○
○

Notes and *shit*

July 2022

4 MONDAY	5 TUESDAY	6 WEDNESDAY
Independence Day (US)		

_____
_____
_____
_____
_____
_____
_____
_____
_____
_____
_____
_____

○ _____
○ _____
○ _____
○ _____
○ _____
○ _____
○ _____
○ _____
○ _____

Important as *fuck*

_____
_____
_____

Fucking grateful for...

_____
_____
_____

Thank you for being fucking awesome

7 THURSDAY	8 FRIDAY	9 SATURDAY

Thursday:
_____
_____
_____
_____
_____
_____
_____
_____
_____
_____
_____
_____
_____
○ _____
○ _____
○ _____
○ _____
○ _____
○ _____
○ _____
○ _____
○ _____

Friday:
_____
_____
_____
_____
_____
_____
_____
_____
_____
○ _____
○ _____
○ _____
○ _____
○ _____
○ _____
○ _____
○ _____
○ _____

Saturday:
_____
_____
_____
_____
_____
_____
○ _____
○ _____
○ _____

10 SUNDAY

_____
_____
_____
_____
_____
_____
○ _____
○ _____
○ _____

Notes and *shit*

_____
_____
_____

July 2022

Important as *fuck*

Fucking grateful for...

You're not bossy. You just have better ideas.

14 THURSDAY

15 FRIDAY

16 SATURDAY

○
○
○

17 SUNDAY

○
○
○
○
○
○
○
○
○

○
○
○
○
○
○
○
○
○

○
○
○

Notes and shit

July 2022

18 MONDAY	19 TUESDAY	20 WEDNESDAY
_____	_____	_____
_____	_____	_____
_____	_____	_____
_____	_____	_____
_____	_____	_____
_____	_____	_____
_____	_____	_____
_____	_____	_____
_____	_____	_____
_____	_____	_____
_____	_____	_____
_____	_____	_____

- ○ _____
- ○ _____
- ○ _____
- ○ _____
- ○ _____
- ○ _____
- ○ _____
- ○ _____
- ○ _____

Important as *fuck*

_____
_____
_____

Fucking grateful for...

_____
_____
_____

Reminder: No one has all their shit together

21 THURSDAY

_____
_____
_____
_____
_____
_____
_____
_____
_____
_____
_____
_____

- ○ _____
- ○ _____
- ○ _____
- ○ _____
- ○ _____
- ○ _____
- ○ _____
- ○ _____
- ○ _____

22 FRIDAY

_____
_____
_____
_____
_____
_____
_____
_____
_____
_____
_____

- ○ _____
- ○ _____
- ○ _____
- ○ _____
- ○ _____
- ○ _____
- ○ _____
- ○ _____
- ○ _____

23 SATURDAY

_____
_____
_____
_____

- ○ _____
- ○ _____
- ○ _____

24 SUNDAY

_____
_____
_____
_____
_____

- ○ _____
- ○ _____
- ○ _____

Notes and shit

_____
_____
_____

July 2022

Don't worry what assholes think...

Important as fuck

_____
_____
_____

Fucking grateful for...

_____
_____
_____

Thinking is not one of their strengths.

28 THURSDAY

29 FRIDAY

30 SATURDAY

○
○
○

31 SUNDAY

28 THURSDAY list:
○
○
○
○
○
○
○
○
○

29 FRIDAY list:
○
○
○
○
○
○
○
○
○

30 SATURDAY / 31 SUNDAY list:
○
○
○

Notes and *shit*

AUGUST 2022

Sunday	Monday	Tuesday	Wednesday
	1	2	3
7	8	9	10
14	15	16	17
21	22	23	24
28	29 Summer Bank Holiday (UK)	30	31

Wake up. Kick ass. Repeat.

Thursday	Friday	Saturday	Important shit
4	5	6	
11	12	13	
18	19	20	
25	26	27	

July

S	M	T	W	T	F	S
					1	2
3	4	5	6	7	8	9
10	11	12	13	14	15	16
17	18	19	20	21	22	23
24	25	26	27	28	29	30
31						

September

S	M	T	W	T	F	S
				1	2	3
4	5	6	7	8	9	10
11	12	13	14	15	16	17
18	19	20	21	22	23	24
25	26	27	28	29	30	

August 2022

1 MONDAY	2 TUESDAY	3 WEDNESDAY

_____

Important as *fuck*

_____

Fucking **grateful for...**

_____

because slapping the shit out of people is frowned upon

4 THURSDAY   5 FRIDAY   6 SATURDAY

_____   _____   _____
_____   _____   _____
_____   _____   _____
_____   _____   _____
_____   _____   _____
_____   _____   _____
_____   _____   ○ _____
_____   _____   ○ _____
_____   _____   ○ _____
_____   _____
_____   _____   7 SUNDAY
_____   _____
_____   _____   _____
○ _____   ○ _____   _____
○ _____   ○ _____   _____
○ _____   ○ _____   _____
○ _____   ○ _____   _____
○ _____   ○ _____
○ _____   ○ _____
○ _____   ○ _____   ○ _____
○ _____   ○ _____   ○ _____
○ _____   ○ _____   ○ _____

Notes and *shit*

_____
_____
_____

August 2022

8 MONDAY	9 TUESDAY	10 WEDNESDAY

Important as *fuck*

Fucking grateful for...

Rise and fucking shine

11 THURSDAY

_____
_____
_____
_____
_____
_____
_____
_____
_____
_____
_____
_____

- ○ _____
- ○ _____
- ○ _____
- ○ _____
- ○ _____
- ○ _____
- ○ _____
- ○ _____
- ○ _____

12 FRIDAY

_____
_____
_____
_____
_____
_____
_____
_____
_____
_____
_____
_____

- ○ _____
- ○ _____
- ○ _____
- ○ _____
- ○ _____
- ○ _____
- ○ _____
- ○ _____
- ○ _____

13 SATURDAY

_____
_____
_____
_____

- ○ _____
- ○ _____
- ○ _____

14 SUNDAY

_____
_____
_____
_____
_____

- ○ _____
- ○ _____
- ○ _____

Notes and shit

_____
_____
_____

August 2022

Kindness is like a boomerang. . .

15 MONDAY	16 TUESDAY	17 WEDNESDAY

_____

Important as fuck

_____

_____

_____

Fucking grateful for...

_____

_____

Throw that shit around and it will come back to you

18 THURSDAY

_____
_____
_____
_____
_____
_____
_____
_____
_____
_____
_____
_____

- ○ _____
- ○ _____
- ○ _____
- ○ _____
- ○ _____
- ○ _____
- ○ _____
- ○ _____
- ○ _____

19 FRIDAY

_____
_____
_____
_____
_____
_____
_____
_____
_____

- ○ _____
- ○ _____
- ○ _____
- ○ _____
- ○ _____
- ○ _____
- ○ _____
- ○ _____
- ○ _____

20 SATURDAY

_____
_____
_____

- ○ _____
- ○ _____
- ○ _____

21 SUNDAY

_____
_____
_____
_____
_____

- ○ _____
- ○ _____
- ○ _____

Notes and shit

_____
_____
_____

August 2022

Don't compare your real life...

22 MONDAY	23 TUESDAY	24 WEDNESDAY

Important as *fuck*

Fucking grateful for...

To someone else's fake ass highlight reel

25 THURSDAY

_____
_____
_____
_____
_____
_____
_____
_____
_____
_____
_____

○ _____
○ _____
○ _____
○ _____
○ _____
○ _____
○ _____
○ _____
○ _____

26 FRIDAY

_____
_____
_____
_____
_____
_____
_____
_____
_____

○ _____
○ _____
○ _____
○ _____
○ _____
○ _____
○ _____
○ _____
○ _____

27 SATURDAY

_____
_____
_____
_____
_____
○ _____
○ _____
○ _____

28 SUNDAY

_____
_____
_____
_____
_____
○ _____
○ _____
○ _____

Notes and shit

_____
_____
_____

SEPTEMBER 2022

Sunday	Monday	Tuesday	Wednesday
August S M T W T F S 1 2 3 4 5 6 7 8 9 10 11 12 13 14 15 16 17 18 19 20 21 22 23 24 25 26 27 28 29 30 31	October S M T W T F S 1 2 3 4 5 6 7 8 9 10 11 12 13 14 15 16 17 18 19 20 21 22 23 24 25 26 27 28 29 30 31		
4	5 Labor Day (US, CA)	6	7
11	12	13	14
18	19	20	21
25	26	27	28

You. Can. Do. This. Shit.

Thursday	Friday	Saturday	Important *shit*
1	2	3	_____
8	9	10	_____
15	16	17	_____
22	23	24	_____
29	30		_____

29 MONDAY	30 TUESDAY	31 WEDNESDAY
Summer Bank Holiday (UK)		

Important as *fuck*

Fucking grateful for...

Look at you kicking ass and shit

1 THURSDAY

_____
_____
_____
_____
_____
_____
_____
_____
_____
_____
_____

- ○ _____
- ○ _____
- ○ _____
- ○ _____
- ○ _____
- ○ _____
- ○ _____
- ○ _____
- ○ _____

2 FRIDAY

_____
_____
_____
_____
_____
_____
_____
_____
_____

- ○ _____
- ○ _____
- ○ _____
- ○ _____
- ○ _____
- ○ _____
- ○ _____
- ○ _____
- ○ _____

3 SATURDAY

_____
_____
_____
_____

- ○ _____
- ○ _____
- ○ _____

4 SUNDAY

_____
_____
_____
_____

- ○ _____
- ○ _____
- ○ _____

Notes and shit

_____
_____
_____

September 2022

If assholes are trying to drag you down. . .

5 MONDAY	6 TUESDAY	7 WEDNESDAY
Labor Day (US, CA)		

Important as fuck

_____

_____

_____

Fucking grateful for...

_____

_____

_____

it just means you're above them

8 THURSDAY	9 FRIDAY	10 SATURDAY

Notes and *shit*

September 2022

12 MONDAY	13 TUESDAY	14 WEDNESDAY
_____	_____	_____
_____	_____	_____
_____	_____	_____
_____	_____	_____
_____	_____	_____
_____	_____	_____
_____	_____	_____
_____	_____	_____
_____	_____	_____
_____	_____	_____
_____	_____	_____
_____	_____	_____
_____	_____	_____

- ◯ _____
- ◯ _____
- ◯ _____
- ◯ _____
- ◯ _____
- ◯ _____
- ◯ _____
- ◯ _____
- ◯ _____

Important as fuck

_____
_____
_____

Fucking grateful for...

_____
_____
_____

Be bold. Be brave. Be your badass self.

15 THURSDAY

_____
_____
_____
_____
_____
_____
_____
_____
_____
_____

○ _____
○ _____
○ _____
○ _____
○ _____
○ _____
○ _____
○ _____
○ _____

16 FRIDAY

_____
_____
_____
_____
_____
_____
_____
_____
_____
_____

○ _____
○ _____
○ _____
○ _____
○ _____
○ _____
○ _____
○ _____
○ _____

17 SATURDAY

_____
_____
_____
_____
○ _____
○ _____
○ _____

18 SUNDAY

_____
_____
_____
_____
_____
○ _____
○ _____
○ _____

Notes and shit

_____
_____
_____

September 2022

Don't take any shit. Take breaks,

19 MONDAY   20 TUESDAY   21 WEDNESDAY

_____   _____   _____
_____   _____   _____
_____   _____   _____
_____   _____   _____
_____   _____   _____
_____   _____   _____
_____   _____   _____
_____   _____   _____
_____   _____   _____
_____   _____   _____
_____   _____   _____
_____   _____   _____

- ⃝ _____   ⃝ _____   ⃝ _____
- ⃝ _____   ⃝ _____   ⃝ _____
- ⃝ _____   ⃝ _____   ⃝ _____
- ⃝ _____   ⃝ _____   ⃝ _____
- ⃝ _____   ⃝ _____   ⃝ _____
- ⃝ _____   ⃝ _____   ⃝ _____
- ⃝ _____   ⃝ _____   ⃝ _____
- ⃝ _____   ⃝ _____   ⃝ _____
- ⃝ _____   ⃝ _____   ⃝ _____

Important as *fuck*

_____
_____
_____

Fucking grateful for...

_____
_____
_____

walks and stuff you need. But don't take any shit.

22 THURSDAY

_____
_____
_____
_____
_____
_____
_____
_____
_____
_____
_____
- ○ _____
- ○ _____
- ○ _____
- ○ _____
- ○ _____
- ○ _____
- ○ _____
- ○ _____
- ○ _____

23 FRIDAY

_____
_____
_____
_____
_____
_____
_____
_____
_____
_____
_____
- ○ _____
- ○ _____
- ○ _____
- ○ _____
- ○ _____
- ○ _____
- ○ _____
- ○ _____
- ○ _____

24 SATURDAY

_____
_____
_____
_____
_____
- ○ _____
- ○ _____
- ○ _____

25 SUNDAY

_____
_____
_____
- ○ _____
- ○ _____
- ○ _____

Notes and *shit*

_____
_____
_____

September-October 2022

26 MONDAY	27 TUESDAY	28 WEDNESDAY
_____	_____	_____
_____	_____	_____
_____	_____	_____
_____	_____	_____
_____	_____	_____
_____	_____	_____
_____	_____	_____
_____	_____	_____
_____	_____	_____
_____	_____	_____
_____	_____	_____
○ _____	○ _____	○ _____
○ _____	○ _____	○ _____
○ _____	○ _____	○ _____
○ _____	○ _____	○ _____
○ _____	○ _____	○ _____
○ _____	○ _____	○ _____
○ _____	○ _____	○ _____
○ _____	○ _____	○ _____
○ _____	○ _____	○ _____

Important as *fuck*

_____

_____

_____

Fucking grateful for...

_____

_____

_____

You swear because you care

29 THURSDAY

_____
_____
_____
_____
_____
_____
_____
_____
_____
_____
_____
_____
_____

○ _____
○ _____
○ _____
○ _____
○ _____
○ _____
○ _____
○ _____
○ _____

30 FRIDAY

_____
_____
_____
_____
_____
_____
_____
_____
_____
_____
_____

○ _____
○ _____
○ _____
○ _____
○ _____
○ _____
○ _____
○ _____
○ _____

1 SATURDAY

_____
_____
_____
_____

○ _____
○ _____
○ _____

2 SUNDAY

_____
_____
_____
_____
_____

○ _____
○ _____
○ _____

Notes and shit

_____
_____
_____

OCTOBER 2022

Sunday	Monday	Tuesday	Wednesday
2	3	4	5
9	10 Columbus Day (US) Thanksgiving (CA)	11	12
16	17	18	19
23	24	25	26
30	31 Halloween		

Keep fucking going

Thursday	Friday	Saturday
		1
6	7	8
13	14	15
20	21	22
27	28	29

Important shit

_____
_____
_____
_____
_____
_____
_____
_____
_____
_____
_____
_____
_____
_____
_____
_____
_____
_____
_____
_____
_____
_____
_____
_____
_____
_____
_____
_____
_____

September

S	M	T	W	T	F	S
				1	2	3
4	5	6	7	8	9	10
11	12	13	14	15	16	17
18	19	20	21	22	23	24
25	26	27	28	29	30	

November

S	M	T	W	T	F	S
		1	2	3	4	5
6	7	8	9	10	11	12
13	14	15	16	17	18	19
20	21	22	23	24	25	26
27	28	29	30			

October 2022

3 MONDAY	4 TUESDAY	5 WEDNESDAY
_____	_____	_____
_____	_____	_____
_____	_____	_____
_____	_____	_____
_____	_____	_____
_____	_____	_____
_____	_____	_____
_____	_____	_____
_____	_____	_____
_____	_____	_____
_____	_____	_____
_____	_____	_____

- ○ _____
- ○ _____
- ○ _____
- ○ _____
- ○ _____
- ○ _____
- ○ _____
- ○ _____
- ○ _____

Important as fuck

_____
_____
_____

Fucking grateful for...

_____
_____

If only closed minds came with closed fucking mouths

6 THURSDAY

_____
_____
_____
_____
_____
_____
_____
_____
_____
_____
_____
_____

○ _____
○ _____
○ _____
○ _____
○ _____
○ _____
○ _____
○ _____
○ _____

7 FRIDAY

_____
_____
_____
_____
_____
_____
_____
_____
_____
_____
_____
_____

○ _____
○ _____
○ _____
○ _____
○ _____
○ _____
○ _____
○ _____
○ _____

8 SATURDAY

_____
_____
_____
_____
_____
○ _____
○ _____
○ _____

9 SUNDAY

_____
_____
_____
_____
_____
○ _____
○ _____
○ _____

Notes and shit

_____
_____
_____

October 2022

10 MONDAY	11 TUESDAY	12 WEDNESDAY
Columbus Day (US), Thanksgiving (CA)		

Important as *fuck*

Fucking grateful for...

about a person and talking truth about a shitty person

13 THURSDAY	14 FRIDAY	15 SATURDAY
_____	_____	_____
_____	_____	_____
_____	_____	_____
_____	_____	_____
_____	_____	_____
_____	_____	_____
_____	_____	○ _____
_____	_____	○ _____
_____	_____	○ _____

16 SUNDAY

○ _____ ○ _____
○ _____ ○ _____ _____
○ _____ ○ _____ _____
○ _____ ○ _____ _____
○ _____ ○ _____ _____
○ _____ ○ _____ _____
○ _____ ○ _____ ○ _____
○ _____ ○ _____ ○ _____
○ _____ ○ _____ ○ _____

Notes and shit

_____

_____

_____

October 2022

17 MONDAY	18 TUESDAY	19 WEDNESDAY
_____	_____	_____
_____	_____	_____
_____	_____	_____
_____	_____	_____
_____	_____	_____
_____	_____	_____
_____	_____	_____
_____	_____	_____
_____	_____	_____
_____	_____	_____
_____	_____	_____
_____	_____	_____
_____	_____	_____
○ _____	○ _____	○ _____
○ _____	○ _____	○ _____
○ _____	○ _____	○ _____
○ _____	○ _____	○ _____
○ _____	○ _____	○ _____
○ _____	○ _____	○ _____
○ _____	○ _____	○ _____
○ _____	○ _____	○ _____
○ _____	○ _____	○ _____

Important as fuck

_____

_____

_____

Fucking grateful for...

_____

_____

_____

You are fucking amazing. —The Universe

20 THURSDAY

_____
_____
_____
_____
_____
_____
_____
_____
_____
_____
_____
_____

- ○ _____
- ○ _____
- ○ _____
- ○ _____
- ○ _____
- ○ _____
- ○ _____
- ○ _____
- ○ _____

21 FRIDAY

_____
_____
_____
_____
_____
_____
_____
_____
_____
_____

- ○ _____
- ○ _____
- ○ _____
- ○ _____
- ○ _____
- ○ _____
- ○ _____
- ○ _____
- ○ _____

22 SATURDAY

_____
_____
_____
_____
_____
- ○ _____
- ○ _____
- ○ _____

23 SUNDAY

_____
_____
_____
_____
_____
- ○ _____
- ○ _____
- ○ _____

Notes and shit

_____
_____
_____

October 2022

24 MONDAY	25 TUESDAY	26 WEDNESDAY
_____	_____	_____
_____	_____	_____
_____	_____	_____
_____	_____	_____
_____	_____	_____
_____	_____	_____
_____	_____	_____
_____	_____	_____
_____	_____	_____
_____	_____	_____
_____	_____	_____
_____	_____	_____

- ○ _____
- ○ _____
- ○ _____
- ○ _____
- ○ _____
- ○ _____
- ○ _____
- ○ _____
- ○ _____

Important as fuck

_____
_____
_____

Fucking grateful for...

_____
_____

Show today who's the fucking boss

27 THURSDAY

_____
_____
_____
_____
_____
_____
_____
_____
_____
_____
_____

○ _____
○ _____
○ _____
○ _____
○ _____
○ _____
○ _____
○ _____
○ _____

28 FRIDAY

_____
_____
_____
_____
_____
_____
_____
_____
_____
_____
_____

○ _____
○ _____
○ _____
○ _____
○ _____
○ _____
○ _____
○ _____
○ _____

29 SATURDAY

_____
_____
_____
_____
_____
○ _____
○ _____
○ _____

30 SUNDAY

_____
_____
_____
_____
_____
○ _____
○ _____
○ _____

Notes and shit

_____
_____
_____

NOVEMBER 2022

Sunday	Monday	Tuesday	Wednesday
		1	2
6	7	8 Election Day (US)	9
13 Remembrance Sunday (UK)	14	15	16
20	21	22	23
27	28	29	30

Keep it classy as fuck

Thursday	Friday	Saturday	Important shit
3	4	5	
10	11 Veterans Day (US) / Remembrance Day (CA, UK)	12	
17	18	19	
24	25 Thanksgiving Day (US)	26	

October

S	M	T	W	T	F	S
						1
2	3	4	5	6	7	8
9	10	11	12	13	14	15
16	17	18	19	20	21	22
23	24	25	26	27	28	29
30	31					

December

S	M	T	W	T	F	S
				1	2	3
4	5	6	7	8	9	10
11	12	13	14	15	16	17
18	19	20	21	22	23	24
25	26	27	28	29	30	31

October-November 2022

31 MONDAY Halloween	1 TUESDAY	2 WEDNESDAY
_____	_____	_____
_____	_____	_____
_____	_____	_____
_____	_____	_____
_____	_____	_____
_____	_____	_____
_____	_____	_____
_____	_____	_____
_____	_____	_____
_____	_____	_____
_____	_____	_____
○ _____	○ _____	○ _____
○ _____	○ _____	○ _____
○ _____	○ _____	○ _____
○ _____	○ _____	○ _____
○ _____	○ _____	○ _____
○ _____	○ _____	○ _____
○ _____	○ _____	○ _____
○ _____	○ _____	○ _____
○ _____	○ _____	○ _____

Important as _fuck_

_____

_____

_____

Fucking grateful for...

_____

_____

_____

When life gives you lemons, throw them at assholes

3 THURSDAY

_____
_____
_____
_____
_____
_____
_____
_____
_____
_____
_____
_____

- ○ _____
- ○ _____
- ○ _____
- ○ _____
- ○ _____
- ○ _____
- ○ _____
- ○ _____
- ○ _____

4 FRIDAY

_____
_____
_____
_____
_____
_____
_____
_____
_____
_____
_____

- ○ _____
- ○ _____
- ○ _____
- ○ _____
- ○ _____
- ○ _____
- ○ _____
- ○ _____
- ○ _____

5 SATURDAY

_____
_____
_____
_____
_____

- ○ _____
- ○ _____
- ○ _____

6 SUNDAY

_____
_____
_____
_____
_____
_____

- ○ _____
- ○ _____
- ○ _____

Notes and shit

_____
_____
_____

November 2022

7 MONDAY	8 TUESDAY	9 WEDNESDAY
	Election Day (US)	

Important as *fuck*

Fucking grateful for...

You can't make everyone fucking happy. You're not a taco.

10 THURSDAY

_____
_____
_____
_____
_____
_____
_____
_____
_____
_____
_____
_____

◯ _____
◯ _____
◯ _____
◯ _____
◯ _____
◯ _____
◯ _____
◯ _____
◯ _____

11 FRIDAY
Veterans Day (US), Remembrance Day (CA, UK)

_____
_____
_____
_____
_____
_____
_____
_____
_____
_____

◯ _____
◯ _____
◯ _____
◯ _____
◯ _____
◯ _____
◯ _____
◯ _____
◯ _____

12 SATURDAY

_____
_____
_____
_____

◯ _____
◯ _____
◯ _____

13 SUNDAY
Remembrance Sunday (UK)

_____
_____
_____
_____

◯ _____
◯ _____
◯ _____

Notes and shit

_____
_____
_____

November 2022

Kill them with kindness. . .

14 MONDAY	15 TUESDAY	16 WEDNESDAY
_____	_____	_____
_____	_____	_____
_____	_____	_____
_____	_____	_____
_____	_____	_____
_____	_____	_____
_____	_____	_____
_____	_____	_____
_____	_____	_____
_____	_____	_____
_____	_____	_____
○ _____	○ _____	○ _____
○ _____	○ _____	○ _____
○ _____	○ _____	○ _____
○ _____	○ _____	○ _____
○ _____	○ _____	○ _____
○ _____	○ _____	○ _____
○ _____	○ _____	○ _____
○ _____	○ _____	○ _____
○ _____	○ _____	○ _____

Important as *fuck*

_____
_____
_____

Fucking grateful for...

_____
_____
_____

Or torture them with sarcasm. You have options.

17 THURSDAY

_____
_____
_____
_____
_____
_____
_____
_____
_____
_____
_____
_____
- ○ _____
- ○ _____
- ○ _____
- ○ _____
- ○ _____
- ○ _____
- ○ _____
- ○ _____
- ○ _____

18 FRIDAY

_____
_____
_____
_____
_____
_____
_____
_____
_____
_____
_____
- ○ _____
- ○ _____
- ○ _____
- ○ _____
- ○ _____
- ○ _____
- ○ _____
- ○ _____
- ○ _____

19 SATURDAY

- ○ _____
- ○ _____
- ○ _____

20 SUNDAY

_____
_____
_____
_____
- ○ _____
- ○ _____
- ○ _____

Notes and shit

_____
_____
_____

November 2022

21 MONDAY	22 TUESDAY	23 WEDNESDAY
_____	_____	_____
_____	_____	_____
_____	_____	_____
_____	_____	_____
_____	_____	_____
_____	_____	_____
_____	_____	_____
_____	_____	_____
_____	_____	_____
_____	_____	_____
_____	_____	_____
_____	_____	_____
_____	_____	_____
○ _____	○ _____	○ _____
○ _____	○ _____	○ _____
○ _____	○ _____	○ _____
○ _____	○ _____	○ _____
○ _____	○ _____	○ _____
○ _____	○ _____	○ _____
○ _____	○ _____	○ _____
○ _____	○ _____	○ _____
○ _____	○ _____	○ _____

Important as *fuck*

_____

_____

_____

Fucking grateful for...

_____

_____

_____

Let your dreams be your fucking wings

24 THURSDAY
Thanksgiving Day (US)

25 FRIDAY

26 SATURDAY

- ○
- ○
- ○

27 SUNDAY

- ○
- ○
- ○
- ○
- ○
- ○
- ○
- ○
- ○

- ○
- ○
- ○
- ○
- ○
- ○
- ○
- ○
- ○

- ○
- ○
- ○

Notes and shit

DECEMBER 2022

Sunday	Monday	Tuesday	Wednesday
November S M T W T F S 　 1 2 3 4 5 6 7 8 9 10 11 12 13 14 15 16 17 18 19 20 21 22 23 24 25 26 27 28 29 30	**January 2023** S M T W T F S 1 2 3 4 5 6 7 8 9 10 11 12 13 14 15 16 17 18 19 20 21 22 23 24 25 26 27 28 29 30 31		
4	5	6	7
11	12	13	14
18 Hanukkah, begins at sundown	19	20	21
25 Christmas Day	26 Boxing Day (CA, UK) Kwanzaa begins (US)	27 Bank Holiday (UK)	28

Finish on a fucking high note

Thursday	Friday	Saturday	Important shit
1	2	3	_____
8	9	10	_____
15	16	17	_____
22	23	24	_____
29	30	31	_____

November-December 2022

Important as *fuck*

Fucking grateful for...

You are a fucking rock star

1 THURSDAY

_____
_____
_____
_____
_____
_____
_____
_____
_____
_____

○ _____
○ _____
○ _____
○ _____
○ _____
○ _____
○ _____
○ _____
○ _____

2 FRIDAY

_____
_____
_____
_____
_____
_____
_____
_____

○ _____
○ _____
○ _____
○ _____
○ _____
○ _____
○ _____
○ _____
○ _____

3 SATURDAY

_____
_____
_____
_____
_____
○ _____
○ _____
○ _____

4 SUNDAY

_____
_____
_____
_____
_____
○ _____
○ _____
○ _____

Notes and shit

_____
_____
_____

December 2022

5 MONDAY	6 TUESDAY	7 WEDNESDAY
_____	_____	_____
_____	_____	_____
_____	_____	_____
_____	_____	_____
_____	_____	_____
_____	_____	_____
_____	_____	_____
_____	_____	_____
_____	_____	_____
_____	_____	_____
_____	_____	_____
_____	_____	_____
_____	_____	_____

- ◯ _____
- ◯ _____
- ◯ _____
- ◯ _____
- ◯ _____
- ◯ _____
- ◯ _____
- ◯ _____
- ◯ _____

Important as fuck

_____
_____
_____

Fucking grateful for...

_____
_____

If only swearing burned calories

8 THURSDAY

_____
_____
_____
_____
_____
_____
_____
_____
_____
_____
_____
_____

- ○ _____
- ○ _____
- ○ _____
- ○ _____
- ○ _____
- ○ _____
- ○ _____
- ○ _____
- ○ _____

9 FRIDAY

_____
_____
_____
_____
_____
_____
_____
_____
_____
_____

- ○ _____
- ○ _____
- ○ _____
- ○ _____
- ○ _____
- ○ _____
- ○ _____
- ○ _____
- ○ _____

10 SATURDAY

_____
_____
_____
_____
_____

- ○ _____
- ○ _____
- ○ _____

11 SUNDAY

_____
_____
_____
_____

- ○ _____
- ○ _____
- ○ _____

Notes and _shit_

_____
_____
_____

December 2022

12 MONDAY	13 TUESDAY	14 WEDNESDAY

Important as *fuck*

Fucking grateful for...

Smile a lot. The assholes hate that.

15 THURSDAY

16 FRIDAY

17 SATURDAY

- ◯
- ◯
- ◯

18 SUNDAY
Hanukkah, begins at sundown

- ◯
- ◯
- ◯

Thursday checklist:
- ◯
- ◯
- ◯
- ◯
- ◯
- ◯
- ◯
- ◯
- ◯

Friday checklist:
- ◯
- ◯
- ◯
- ◯
- ◯
- ◯
- ◯
- ◯
- ◯

Notes and *shit*

December 2022

19 MONDAY	20 TUESDAY	21 WEDNESDAY
_____	_____	_____
_____	_____	_____
_____	_____	_____
_____	_____	_____
_____	_____	_____
_____	_____	_____
_____	_____	_____
_____	_____	_____
_____	_____	_____
_____	_____	_____
_____	_____	_____
_____	_____	_____
_____	_____	_____
○ _____	○ _____	○ _____
○ _____	○ _____	○ _____
○ _____	○ _____	○ _____
○ _____	○ _____	○ _____
○ _____	○ _____	○ _____
○ _____	○ _____	○ _____
○ _____	○ _____	○ _____
○ _____	○ _____	○ _____
○ _____	○ _____	○ _____

Important as *fuck*

_____

_____

_____

Fucking grateful for...

_____

_____

_____

Way to keep it fucking real

22 THURSDAY

_____
_____
_____
_____
_____
_____
_____
_____
_____
_____
_____
_____

○ _____
○ _____
○ _____
○ _____
○ _____
○ _____
○ _____
○ _____
○ _____

23 FRIDAY

_____
_____
_____
_____
_____
_____
_____
_____
_____

○ _____
○ _____
○ _____
○ _____
○ _____
○ _____
○ _____
○ _____
○ _____

24 SATURDAY

_____
_____
_____
_____
_____
_____

○ _____
○ _____
○ _____

25 SUNDAY
Christmas Day

_____
_____
_____
_____
_____

○ _____
○ _____
○ _____

Notes and shit

_____
_____
_____

December 2022-January 2023

26 MONDAY	27 TUESDAY	28 WEDNESDAY
Boxing Day (CA, UK)	Bank Holiday (UK)	

Important as *fuck*

Fucking grateful for...

You are amazing as fuck. Keep that shit up.

29 THURSDAY

_____
_____
_____
_____
_____
_____
_____
_____
_____
_____
_____

- ○ _____
- ○ _____
- ○ _____
- ○ _____
- ○ _____
- ○ _____
- ○ _____
- ○ _____
- ○ _____

30 FRIDAY

_____
_____
_____
_____
_____
_____
_____
_____
_____
_____
_____

- ○ _____
- ○ _____
- ○ _____
- ○ _____
- ○ _____
- ○ _____
- ○ _____
- ○ _____
- ○ _____

31 SATURDAY

_____
_____
_____
_____
_____

- ○ _____
- ○ _____
- ○ _____

1 SUNDAY
New Year's Day

_____
_____
_____
_____
_____

- ○ _____
- ○ _____
- ○ _____

Notes and shit

_____
_____
_____

My Brilliant Thoughts & Shit

My Brilliant Thoughts & Shit

My Brilliant Thoughts & Shit

My Brilliant Thoughts & Shit

My Brilliant Thoughts & Shit

My Brilliant Thoughts & Shit

My Brilliant Thoughts & Shit

My Brilliant Thoughts & Shit

Thank you for trying us out!

One last reminder:

You are amazing and deserve to be happy as fuck!

Have comments or questions about our books? Want freebies to brighten your day?

Please email us at
sassyquotespress@gmail.com

For more sarcastic planners, journals and coloring books, please visit

https://www.amazon.com/~/e/B08TGS2ZBL

Favor please :)

Would you take a quick minute to leave us a rating/review on Amazon? It makes a HUGE difference and we would really appreciate it.

THANK YOU!

Printed in Great Britain
by Amazon

71416349R00086